Critters, Creatures, and Kelp

A Guide to Life in the Edmonds Underwater Park

Dan Clements

ISBN 9780615267739

www.critterscreaturesandkelp.com

© 2009, All Rights Reserved

Please report new sitings to:

info@critterscreaturesandkelp.com

Printed in Bellevue, Washington, USA by CCS Printing

Edmonds Underwater Park

Table of Contents

Thanks! 3

About the Park and this Guide 4
    Park History 4
    Park Safety 5
    The Altered View Underwater 6
    The Bruce Higgins Trail System 7
    Underwater Trail Map 8

Warm Bodied Critters 9
    Human Beings 10
    River Otter 11
    California Sea Lion 12
    Harbor Seal 13
    Gray Whale 14

Bony & Ratfish Critters 15
    Cabezon 16
    Wattled Eelpouts 17
    Bay Goby 18
    Blackeye Goby 19
    Painted Greenling 20
    Long Fin Gunnel 21
    Pacific Herring 23
    Lingcod 24
    Pile Perch 25
    Shiner Perch 26
    Quillfish 27
    Spotted Ratfish 28
    Red Irish Lord 29
    Black Rockfish 30
    Canary Rockfish 31
    China Rockfish 32
    Copper Rockfish 33
    Humpy or Pink Salmon 34
    Coho or Silver Salmon 35
    Pacific Sand Lance 36
    Speckled Sanddab 37
    Buffalo Sculpin 38
    Grunt Sculpin 39
    Sailfin Sculpin 40
    Scalyhead Sculpin 41
    Striped Seaperch 42
    Longnose Skate 43
    Rock Sole 44
    Tube-snout 45
    Decorated Warbonnet 46

Barnacle, Crab, Lobster, & Shrimp Creatures 47
    Acorn, or Giant Acorn, Barnacle 48
    Decorator Crab 49

Edmonds Underwater Park

    Dungeness Crab 50
    Hermit Crab 51
    Kelp Crab 52
    Red Rock Crab 53
    Squat Lobster 54
    Coonstripe or Dock Shrimp 55
    Ghost Shrimp 56
    Spot Shrimp 57

Chitons, Clams, Mussels, Scallops, & Snail Creatures..................... 58
    Blue Line Chiton 59
    Gumboot Chiton 60
    Hairy Chiton 61
    Lined Chiton 62
    Mossy Chiton 63
    Butter or Long Neck Clam 64
    Geoduck Clam 65
    Horse Clam 66
    Pacific Little Neck Clam 67
    Heart Cockle 68
    California Mussel 69
    Pacific Blue Mussel 70
    Rough Piddock 71
    Rock Scallop 72
    Lewis' Moon Snail 73

Octopi & Squid Critters 74
    Giant Pacific Octopus 75
    Red Octopus 76
    Stubby Squid 77
    Opal Squid 78

Sea Stars, Urchins, & Sea Cucumber Critters................................. 79
    Sea Cucumber 80
    Leather Star 81
    Pacific Blood Star 82
    Purple or Ochre Star 83
    Rose Star 84
    Spiney Red Star 85
    Striped Sun Star 86
    Sunflower Star 87
    Vermilion Star 88
    Green Sea Urchin 89

Anemones, Jellies, & Sea Pen Creatures 90
    Brooding Anemone 91
    Giant Green or Green Surf Anemone 92
    Painted Anemone 93
    Plumose Anemone 94
    Short Plumose Anemone 95
    Tube Anemone 96
    Fried Egg or Egg Yolk Jelly 97
    Lion's Mane Jelly 98
    Sarisa Jelly 99
    Water Jelly 100
    Sea Pen 101

Sea Slug & Worm Creatures 102
    Gold Dirona 104
    Alabaster or White Line Nudibranch 105
    Brown Striped Nudibranch 106
    Hooded or Lion's Mane Nudibranch 107
    Opalescent or Horned Nudibranch 108
    Shaggy or Mouse Nudibranch 109
    Monterey Sea Lemon Nudibranch 110
    Nanaimo Nudibranch 111
    Ring Spotted Nudibranch 112
    Diamond Back Tritonia 113
    Spotted Aglajid 114
    Breadcrumb Sponge 115
    Phyllodoce Scaleworm 116
    Calcareous Tube Worm 117
    Feather Duster Worm 118
    Orange Ribbon Worm 119
    Six Lined Ribbon Worm 120

Eelgrass, Seaweed, and Kelp 121
    Eelgrass 122
    Bull Kelp 123
    Seersucker Kelp 124
    Sugar Kelp or Sugar Wrack 125
    Delicate Sea Lace 126
    Sea Lettuce 127
    Blue Branching Seaweed 128
    Succulent Seaweed 129
    Hairy Pottery Seaweed 130
    Wireweed 131

Bibliography 132
Index 133
Dan Clements 135

THANKS!

This book would not have been possible without assistance from many individuals. Thanks to my dive buddies Jay Sprenger, Bobby Berensen, Jerry Effenberger, and others who took time to help point out photo subjects and buddy with me.

Thanks to fellow photographers Johanna Raupe, Veronica von Allwörden, Rhoda Green, and Pat Gunderson. Also many thanks to government photographers and those who submitted pictures and information to Wikipedia for public use.

Most of all, thanks to Bruce Higgins, the City of Edmonds, and the legion of volunteers who have made the Edmonds Underwater Park happen.

About the Park and this Guide

My first dive in the Edmonds Underwater Park was a literal eye opener. Having worked on hiking and mountain bike trails, I have a good understanding of the labor needed to construct and maintain trail systems.

What I initially saw was a sophisticated underwater park that involved thousands of hours of delicate and complicated labor to create. Trails laid out on magnetic compass headings, concrete and other features designed to provide habitat for marine life, sunken boats and dry docks teeming with wildlife.

And what wildlife! On the way to the trails you swim over the many sea star, moon snails, and Dungeness crab. On the trail system we pass large cabezon and lingcod guarding their nests.

Then the smaller critters, beautiful nudibranchs and small jellies catch your attention. This is a unique site to observe and interact with Puget Sound sea life. So how did this Park come to be?

Park History

Dating to 1970, the 27 acre Edmonds Underwater Park appears to be the second oldest municipal dive park in the United States. The Casino Underwater Park on Catalina Island was established approximately a decade earlier.

After a series of dive related fatalities in the mid-1970's, there was much discussion in the City about the Park's future. The dive park had several champions on the city council, and in 1977 a young marine biologist named Bruce Higgins joined the committee established to improve diver safety. Bruce then participated in drafting a management plan for the Park.

In the past 30 years Bruce and some 350 other volunteers have logged over 25,000 hours of dive time in the Park. Today there are over two miles of marked trails that run in a magnetic north/south, east/west pattern. There are numerous man made features: sunken boats, railroad tie pyramid, concrete structures, and habitat for many different types of marine critters and creatures.

Bruce and the volunteer force supporting the Park have created a world class dive park. The availability of food and habitat has created an environment where life thrives. The Park is truly unique in that it is possible to observe many species nesting and swimming literally on trail lines and markers.

In recognition of the work Bruce has done over the past 30 years, on July 7, 2007 the City of Edmonds formally renamed the trail system the Bruce Higgins Underwater Trails.

Park Safety

The Edmonds Underwater Park is generally a very safe environment for divers. Maximum depths are less than 45 feet. The two main considerations are current and visibility.

Puget Sound can see tidal exchanges in excess of 15 feet. This can produce strong currents. It is safest to dive around slack tide, or at times when there is minimal tidal exchange.

Visibility in the Park can range from over 30 feet to less than a foot. From late April to August the long days result in plankton blooms that restrict visibility.

Strong rains and run-off wash sediment into the water that can restrict visibility at any time of the year. Be sure to bring a compass and know how to navigate underwater. The trail system is a great help, but it is not a substitute for basic navigation skills.

The City of Edmonds has adopted a simple set of rules to help insure the safety of all those who use the Park. These include: 1.) No solo diving, always dive with a buddy; 2.) No boats, including motorized underwater equipment, are allowed in the Park; 3.) Keep at least 300 feet away from the ferry terminal; and 4.) Keep well away from ferries, which are known in the vernacular as "Diver Grinders."

The Altered View Underwater

On your first few dives in the Edmonds Underwater Park the flora and fauna may seem washed out. Why is this?

As you descend deeper into Puget Sound water absorbs the red and yellow light spectrums. Consequently, plants and animals appear washed out, looking bluish and dull.

To compensate for this, photographers use strobes and flashes, while divers use lights to reveal beautiful colors of the critters, creatures, and kelp that call the Edmonds Underwater Park their home.

Bruce Higgins, 2008

The Bruce Higgins Trail System

The following page provides a simple map of the Park's trail system. More detailed maps, showing Park features like sunken boats, and man-made objects can be purchased at Edmonds Underwater Sports, a few hundred yards south of the Park.

So what are underwater trails? Bruce and his legion of volunteers have placed cinder blocks on the sea bed, and run various types of rope through them.

I hope you enjoy the Edmonds Underwater Park and Bruce Higgins Trail system as much as I do. Hopefully this book will enhance your enjoyment!

- Dan Clements

Bruce Higgins Underwater Trails

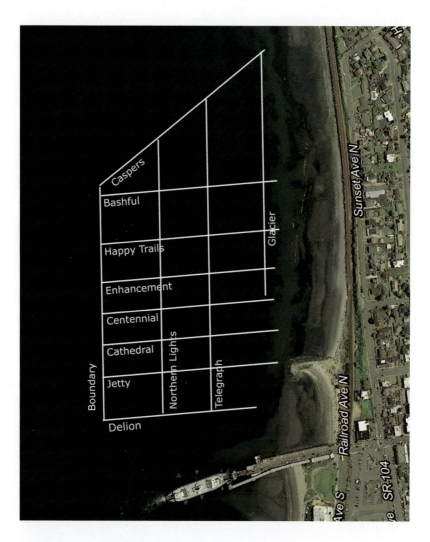

The Bruce Higgins trail system greatly simplifies underwater navigation. Trails run magnetic north to south and magnetic east to west. There is no need to adjust for magnetic declination.

Warm Bodied Critters

Human Beings
Homo sapien scubenses

Bobby Berensen by Dan Clements

Size: To 80 inches (203 centimeters)

Human Beings are a common, non-native species in the Edmonds Underwater Park. They can be found in all areas, at all depths.

On one hand, this species has the ability to carefully observe, manage, and develop the Park. On the other, this species can damage and destroy other species and habitat.

Please dive and explore responsibly: leave only bubbles, take only pictures.

River Otter
Lontra canadensis

Dan Clements

Size: To 50 inches (127 centimeters)

Although called a river otter, these animals are found in both marine and freshwater habitats throughout Puget Sound. Unlike sea otters, river otters bring their prey ashore to eat.

Their diet consists of fish, small crustaceans, insects, and small mammals. They generally hunt at night, or during twilight.

These animals are not commonly seen in the Park.

California Sea Lion
Zalophus californianus

David Ball, Wikipedia

Size: To 8 feet (2.4 meters)

California sea lions are infrequent visitors: usually passing though on their way to other parts of Puget Sound where they "raft" up and join other sea lions.

These are very intelligent, highly social marine animals. They are opportunistic feeders, and will feast on most squid, octopus, herring, rockfish, mackerel, and other fish found in the Park.

Males may weigh up to 1,000 pounds, and have a pronounced ridge on their skulls.

Harbor Seal
Phoca vitulina

Clark Anderson, Wikipedia

Size: To 72 inches (183 centimeters)

Harbor seals are fairly regular visitors. Naturally inquisitive, they will often swim up to, and examine divers. They have been known to playfully nibble on fins and use lights on night dives to locate prey.

Unlike sea lions, harbor seals are more solitary and do not live in large colonies. They are fond of eating the Park's crab, shrimp, clams, and fish. Like many teenagers, they do not chew their food: they either swallow it whole, or tear it into large pieces.

Gray Whale
Eschrichtius robustus

Veronica von Allwörden, Sky and Sea Photography

Size: To 52 feet (16 meters)

Although not common in the Park, every year or two a gray whale swims through, frequently rolling on its right side to scoop up bottom sediment and snack on small shrimp and other bottom dwelling crustaceans.

Gray whales have the longest migration of any mammal: 12,500 miles from Alaska to Baja California.

These whales are renowned for their "fish" breath. When they exhale through their blowholes, beach watchers have been known to head for cover.

Bony & Rat Fish Critters

For Additional Information:

On-line:
www.fishbase.org

Print:
Coastal Fish Identification
California to Alaska by Paul Humann

Cabezon
Scorpaenichthys marmoratus

Dan Clements

Size: To 30 inches (76 centimeters)

Cabezon is Spanish for "big head," and this is one of the distinguishing characteristics of this critter. Cabezon are common in the Park. Males sit on and guard nests. They will frequently charge and bump divers. Since they have no dangerous teeth, gently push them away if they charge.

While cabezon do not bite, their eggs are toxic to humans and other mammals, and their sharp spines can easily pass through neoprene gloves. They can live 20 years, and eat other fish, crab, and molluscs.

Wattled Eelpout
Lycodes palearis

NOAA- Alaska Fisheries Science Center

Size: To 20.1 inches (51 centimeters)

Wattled eelpouts are rare visitors to the Park. They typically like deeper water. They prefer sandy bottoms where they can feed on small shrimp and molluscs. In turn, they are on the dinner menu for mammals such as sea lions and larger fish.

This is one of four eelpouts found in Puget Sound, and it is the largest. Wattled Eelpouts spawn from December through February.

Bay Goby
Lepidogobius lepidus

Clinton Bauder

Size: To 3.9 inches (10 centimeters)

Bay gobies range along the Pacific Coast from Northern British Columbia to Central Baja California. They may be found on sandy and muddy bottom throughout the Park. They have a life span up to seven years.

Their home is a burrow or den in the sand or bottom material. Females lay their eggs and they are attached to the walls of the burrow. These fish spawn year round, peaking in late spring.

Blackeye Goby
Coryphopterus nicholsii

Dan Clements

Size: To 5.9 inches (15 centimeters)

Blackeye gobies are one of the Park's "polygamists." They form "harem" groups consisting of one male and several smaller females.

They have a lifespan of approximately 4.5 years, and are found in sandy areas next to the Park's rocks and man made concrete features. Their diet includes plankton, small molluscs, and marine invertebrates.

Home for these fish can be burrows in the sand, dens in rocky areas, or inside bottles or pipes.

Painted Greenling
Oxylebius pictus

Dan Clements

Size: To 9.8 inches (25 centimeters)

Painted greenling are quite common throughout the Park. If you look closely, you will be able to see cirri, or what look like horns, above each eye, and between the eyes and dorsal fin.

They live a maximum of eight years, and have an interesting bed: sleeping on an anemone and returning nightly.

They eat small crustaceans, worms, and other invertebrates.

Long Fin Gunnel
Pholis clemensi

Johanna Raupe

Size: To 5 inches (12.7 centimeters)

At five inches, this is the smallest member of the gunnel family found in the Park. With their reddish/orange color, they provide striking contrast to the leafy algae they like to inhabit. Look for them on rock and man-made concrete structures. On occasion you can see them swimming.

These are shy fish that are wary of divers. On rare occasions they will look out from their hiding areas and feel comfortable enough to let people approach. They dine on small shellfish.

Saddleback Gunnel
Pholis ornate

Dan Clements

Size: To 12 inches (30.5 centimeters)

Saddleback gunnels are striking eel-like fish that are rarely seen by divers. Their habitat is most commonly on the muddy and sandy bottom in eelgrass and seaweed.

They are most active at night, and are quite skittish when approached. They use small nooks and crannies, bottles, cans, and open pipe as their dens.

Their diet consists of small crustaceans and molluscs.

Pacific Herring
Clupea pallasii

Mary Whalen, USGS

Size: To 18 inches (46 centimeters)

Pacific herring are common throughout the Edmonds Underwater Park. They are plankton feeders and are on the frequent dining list for larger fish and salmon, seals, seabirds, and man.

Spawning normally occurs in marine vegetation close to shore where fertilized eggs attach to plants like eelgrass. The Pacific herring fisheries collapsed in 1993, and has been slowly re-establishing itself. Major reasons cited for the decline are over fishing and environmental degradation.

Lingcod
Ophiodon elongates

Dan Clements

Size: To 72 inches (183 centimeters)

Lingcod are the largest fish seen in the Park. Living up to 20 years, they can grow to approximately six feet and weigh 130 pounds. They are quite used to divers, and can be approached very closely.

They are common throughout the Park, and enjoy resting on jetty rocks, concrete trail markings, and on sunken boats.

Their primary diet includes other fish, octopi, squid, and crustaceans.

Pile Perch
Rhacochilus vacca

Dan Clements

Size: To 17.3 inches (44 centimeters)

Pile perch are common in the Park, but are most frequently seen in and around the eelgrass. They can sometimes be seen in large schools.

They enjoy dining on crab, hard shelled molluscs, and barnacles. They can live up to ten years.

While adult pile perch are large enough to avoid most predators, they are listed as having moderate to high vulnerability due to excessive commercial and sport fishing.

Shiner Perch
Cymatogaster aggregata

Dan Clements

Size: To 8 inches (20 centimeters)

The beautifully reflective shiner perch enjoy the shallow water found near the Park's eelgrass beds. When schooling in deeper waters they provide beautiful surfaces for sunlight to reflect off.

These fish live up to nine years. They are preyed upon by seals, sea lion, river otter, and larger fish. Their diet consists of small crustaceans, clams, and other bivalves.

Quillfish
Ptilichthys goodei

G Brown Goode, Wikipedia

Size: 13.4 inches (34 centimeters)

This eel looking fish is rarely seen, and little is known about its life span, diet, and activities. When it is spotted, it is at night, where it is attracted by diving lights.

Several references indicate that the fish may dig into the sea floor during the day, and emerge to hunt during the nighttime darkness.

Quillfish remains have been found in the stomachs of coho and chinook salmon.

Spotted Ratfish
Hydrolagus colliei

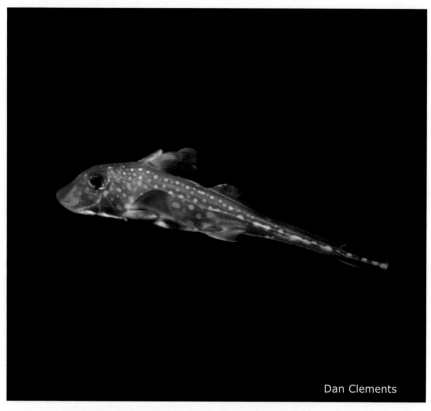

Dan Clements

Size: To 38 inches (96.5 centimeters)

Spotted ratfish are related to sharks and skates. Since ratfish contain both cartilage and bone, they are sometimes referred to as the link between these two major fish groups. They can live to 14 years.

They are most commonly seen at night gliding over the bottom searching for prey. They prefer crab, clams, worms, and small fish.

They are named after the rat tail like appearance of their tails.

Red Irish Lord
Hemilepidotus hemilepidotus

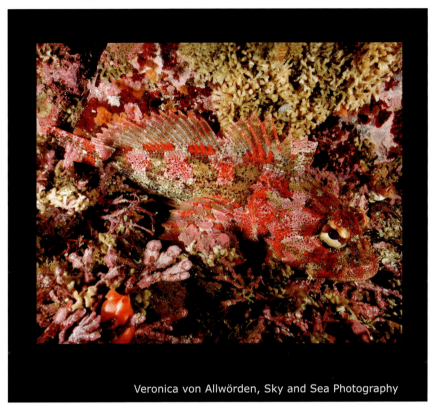

Veronica von Allwörden, Sky and Sea Photography

Size: Up to 20.1 inches (51 centimeters)

These colorful fish rest on the bottom and are well camouflaged among the anemones, pink algae, and plants that surround them.

Red Irish Lords are classic ambush hunters. They wait until prey passes in close proximity and then "pounce." They enjoy dining on small crustaceans, molluscs, snails, worms, and smaller fish.

In order to help with their hunting, they have the ability to change color to match their surroundings.

Black Rockfish
Sebastes melanops

Dan Clements

Size: Up to 24 inches (61 centimeters)

Black rockfish are among the longest lived creatures in the Park. They can live up to 50 years.

Adults are large enough to avoid most predators, but both seals and humans place them high on the dining menu. They have a broad diet consisting of small crustaceans, shrimp, smaller fish, worms, and sponges. Young Black Rockfish are an important source of food for other fish, birds, and marine mammals. Look for these fish near the Park's many man-made features.

Canary Rockfish
Sebastes pinniger

Stan Shebs, Wikipedia

Size: To 29 inches (73.7 centimeters)

Living up to 84 years, canary rockfish earn the title of the Park's most senior fish citizen. These fish are highly vulnerable due to overfishing by commercial and sport interests.

They feed on small fish and krill. Because of their size they are food for marine mammals such as seals and man.

They can be seen throughout the Park, but are most commonly seen hovering near man-made objects.

China Rockfish
Sebastes nebulosus

Stan Shebs, Wikipedia

Size: Up to 17 inches (43.2 centimeters)

With a life span of up to 79 years, China rockfish live longer than most humans. They are also "homebodies" who spend their lives in the same locale for years. They like to hide in nooks and crannies found in many of the Park's features.

These spectacular speckled, black and yellow fish have mildly poisonous spines. Their diet is quite broad, ranging from squid to crab, to sea stars, molluscs, to smaller fish.

Copper Rockfish
Sebastes caurinus

Dan Clements

Size: To 22 inches (55.9 centimeters)

Copper rockfish can live as long as 40 years. Their habitat is generally close to the bottom, where they favor pebbly and rocky composition over sand. They are common throughout the Park, and are frequently seen in and around the many man-made features and sunken boats.

These fish eat small fish, shrimp, squid, octopi, and crabs, and are in turn one of the favorite dishes for lingcod, cabezon, and fishermen.

Humpy or Pink Salmon
Oncorhynchus gorbuscha

E R Keeley, USGS

Size: To 30 inches (76 centimeters)

Pink or humpback salmon are the smallest and most numerous species of Pacific salmon. They live for two years. After hatching, the fry swim from streams and lakes into Puget Sound and the Pacific Ocean. They return two years later to spawn and die. Males grow a large hump on their backs during their spawning migration.

They have a wide diet consisting of insects, fish, squid, crustaceans, and fish eggs. They are preyed upon by orcas, sea lions, sharks, rays, and man.

Coho or Silver Salmon
Oncorhynchus kisutch

Dan Clements

Size: Up to 38.5 inches (97.8 centimeters)

These remarkable fish begin life in fresh water streams, then migrate out into the Pacific Ocean. They return to the stream location where they were hatched, spawn once, and die.

With a life span of approximately four to five years, their diet while young and living in fresh water is primarily insects. As young fish move into Puget Sound their diet changes to plankton and small crustaceans. Their diet in the Pacific consists of prey like jellies, squid, and small fish.

Pacific Sand Lance
Ammodytes hexapterus

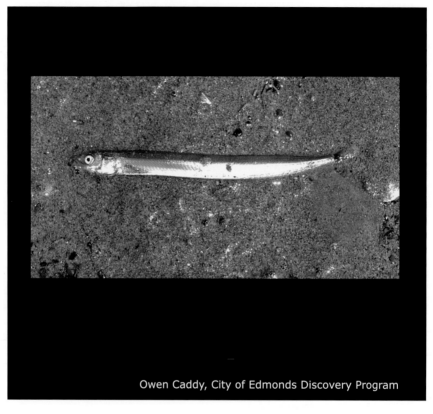

Owen Caddy, City of Edmonds Discovery Program

Size: Up to 11.8 inches (30 centimeters)

The Pacific sand lance is an important food for seabirds, marine mammals, and larger fish, and has a life span up to eleven years.

This fish lives close to shore, and buries itself in the sandy ocean floor. When not buried in sand, they swim with hundreds to thousands of other sand lance in large schools. These large schools brilliantly reflect sunlight off their silver bodies.

Its diet consists of plankton and detritis in the water.

Speckled Sanddab
Citharichthys stigmaeus

Dan Clements

Size: Up to 6.7 inches (17 centimeters)

These flounder type fish with both eyes on one side are found throughout the Park's sandy bottom areas at shallow depths around 15 feet.

The speckled sanddab's diet consists of worms, small crustaceans, and small fish. In turn, its predators are sharks, rays, and seabirds.

This fish is also able to camouflage itself by changing its appearance to match its background.

Buffalo Sculpin
Enophrys bison

Patricia Gunderson

Size: 14.5 inches (37 centimeters)

Buffalo sculpin are found throughout the Park's sandy and rocky bottom areas. Their diet consists of algae, shrimp, crab, mussel, and smaller fish. They are a common prey of harbor seals.

A female will lay from 19,000 to 32,000 orange-brown eggs when they spawn. These egg nests can be seen on rocks and man-made structures in February and March. Males guard the nests, which may contain eggs from multiple females. These fish also change color to match their environment.

Grunt Sculpin
Rhamphocottus richardsonii

Johanna Raupe

Size: 3.5 inches (8.9 centimeters)

Grunt sculpin are the Park's "Sadie Hawkins." During mating season females chase males into crevices on rocks and features until her eggs are fertilized.

For shelter these fish like empty shells, cans, bottles, and the ends of tubing or pipe. They feed on small crustaceans, plankton, and larvae from fish and invertebrates.

Grunt sculpins may also be seen walking over sand and seaweed on their sharp pectoral fins.

Sailfin Sculpin
Nautichthys oculofasciatus

Johanna Raupe

Size: 7.9 inches (20 centimeters)

These unusual fish are rarely seen during the day: they are most active in the Park during nocturnal hours.

Divers have reported seeing this sculpin waving its sail as a way of distracting and confusing prey before it strikes. Its diet consists of small fish and crustaceans.

It prefers areas near rocky bottoms with algae, and lives in crevices in rock and man-made features.

Scalyhead Sculpin
Artedius harringtoni

Dan Clements

Size: 4 inches (10.1 centimeters)

Little is known about the longevity of this common member of the sculpin family, ranging from Alaska to Washington.

The species favors rocky outcroppings and many of the Park's features that are shallower than 20 feet. Like its relatives, it eats worms, molluscs, and small crustaceans. It is preyed upon by larger fish.

Males are quite territorial, and aggressively guard egg nests.

Striped Seaperch
Embiotoca lateralis

Dan Clements

Size: To 15 inches (38.1 centimeters)

Striped seaperch can live up to ten years, and their favorite habitat are the Park's eelgrass and kelp areas. They are a colorful and common sight.

Unlike many creatures in the Park, females do not lay eggs: they are retained within their bodies and they give birth to live babies (ovoviviparous).

While they are on the menu for larger fish and mammals, they dine on crab, shrimp, prawns, molluscs, and algae.

Longnose Skate
Raja rhina

Dan Clements

Size: 24 inches (61 centimeters)

With only its eyes protruding above the sand, this bottom dwelling fish is difficult to spot when it is buried in the sandy bottom areas of the Park. It is much more easily seen when swimming by gracefully undulating its "wings."

It is unclear how long these fish live, but some have been documented to survive 13 years. Skates feed by pinning crustaceans, molluscs, and worms on the sea floor and then eating them. Divers often see a cloud of silt and sand kicked up during meal time.

Rock Sole
Lepidopsetta bilineata

Veronica von Allwörden, Sky and Sea Photography

Size: 23.6 inches (60 centimeters)

Rock sole prefer the Parks sandy, flat bottom areas. Unlike other flatfish they rarely bury themselves and infrequently lie flat. Instead, they sit on the bottom propped up by their fins.

These flatfish have a life expectancy up to 22 years, and are highly vulnerable because of commercial fishing. Their diet consists of fish, worms, molluscs, crustaceans, and brittle stars. Predators include larger fish and man.

Tube-snout
Aulorhynchus flavidus

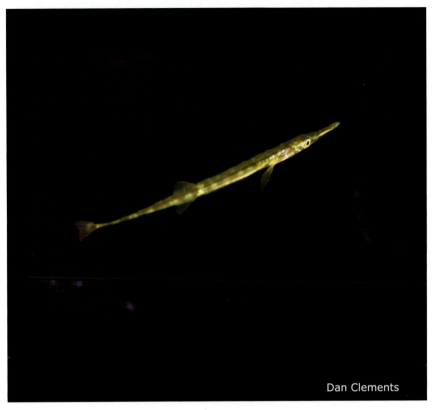

Size: 7.1 inches (18 centimeters)

The tube-snout is a rare visitor to the Pacific Coast from Sitka south to Baja California. It is, however, a fairly common site in the Edmonds Underwater Park.

It favors eelgrass beds where it feeds on small crustaceans, worms, plankton, and fish larvae. They are a food source for larger fish, and can live nine years. During late spring and summer males construct nests of seaweed where numerous females deposit eggs. A single male fertilizes and guards the nest.

Decorated Warbonnet
Chirolophis decoratus

Johanna Raupe

Size: 16.5 inches (42 centimeters)

These spectacularly colored and outfitted fish have a lifespan of some 14 years, and frequent crevices found in rocks, man-made features, and sunken boats. They like to be in close proximity to algae and seaweed.

Decorated warbonnets are quite shy, and will frequently quickly swim into the rocky dens or hiding places when approached by divers. Once frightened they will remain hidden for extended periods.

Barnacle, Crab, Lobster, & Shrimp Creatures

For Additional Information:

On-line:
  http://en.wikipedia.org/
  http://www.sealifebase.org/

Print:
  Whales to Whelks by Rick Harbo
  Marine Life of the Pacific Northwest
    by Andy Lamb

Acorn, or Giant Acorn, Barnacle
Balanus nubilis

Dan Clements

Size: To 6 inches (15 centimeters)

Giant barnacles are filter feeders who enjoy dining on plankton or suspended organic matter floating in the water.

These barnacles are related to shrimp, and their feathery legs act as small nets to capture food. If exposed at low tide, the legs are withdrawn into the shell to conserve moisture.

Giant barnacles are most frequently found on the rocks that make up the jetty.

Decorator Crab
Oregonia gracilis

Dan Clements

Size: 1.5 inches (39 millimeters)

These small crabs are the Park's fashion mavens. They clip off material surrounding them and attach it to their shells. They live up to 10 years.

While these crab grow, their shells do not. Consequently, they molt and lose their old shells and grow new ones. They decorate their new shell with the living organisms and material from their old shells. The decorator crab is on the meal list of numerous fish, especially cabezon, and eats algae, sponge, and small crustaceans.

Dungeness Crab
Cancer magister

Dan Clements

Size: 9 inches (23 centimeters)

Dungeness crab can live up to 13 years, and are common throughout the Park, especially in eelgrass and sandy areas. These large, meaty specimen are the most important commercial crab in the northwest.

Prior to mating, Dungeness engage in an embrace that lasts for several days: they join abdomen to abdomen, face to face. While Dungeness prefer to eat clams, small fish, and other crustaceans, they also scavenge meals.

Hermit Crab
Pagurus beringanus

Dan Clements

Size: To 5.6 inches (14.2 centimeters)

Hermit crabs are actually not true crabs: they have ten legs and are more closely related to shrimp. Some species of hermit crab can live 30 plus years.

As they molt and grow they move into larger shells, and they live in fairly large groups. They are common throughout the Park, and can be found in small shells and large moon snail dwellings.

They are scavengers who eat both plants and detritus. They are eaten by larger fish.

Kelp Crab
Pugettia gracilis

Dan Clements

Size: 8 inches (20 centimeters)

This common crab has a body that is longer than wide, and measures about four inches. Its long legs are quite flexible, and can reach above and behind for defense.

Kelp crabs are commonly seen in the Park clinging onto kelp, seaweed, or features with their rear legs while they grab kelp and detritus with their claws for meals.

Rick Harbo says these are a favorite otter food.

Red Rock Crab
Cancer productus

Kirt L. Onthank, Wikipedia

Size: Body to 7 inches (18 centimeters)

Red rock crab have extremely strong claws that can easily pierce through neoprene gloves. They have a life span of up to seven years, and are most commonly seen in the eelgrass.

This crab is a meat eater, and uses the crushing power of its claws to break open the shells of mussels, clams, snails, and barnacles to get at the morsels inside.

This crab is most active at night.

Squat Lobster
Munida quadrispina

Olympic Coast Preserve, NOAA

Size: Body to 2.6 inches (6.7 centimeters)

Squat lobsters can be seen swimming over muddy bottoms. When resting, they favor rocks or man-made concrete surfaces.

They eat small plankton and the remains of other animals floating through the water. In turn, they are food for marine mammals, octopus, and squid.

Besides being able to swim, they have three pairs of legs for walking, and two claws for catching and tearing food.

Coonstripe or Dock Shrimp
Pandalus danae

Dan Clements

Size: 5.5 inches (14 centimeters)

These shrimp are common throughout the Park and are quite active during the daylight hours. They can be seen darting through the kelp, or hiding in crevices or beneath algae.

They live for approximately three years, and are extremely important for both commercial and sport fisheries. Their favorite food are worms (polychaetes). These critters have an interesting sex life in that individuals spend the early part of life as males, and later transform into females.

Ghost or Sand Shrimp
Callianassa californiensis

Hans Hillewaert, Wikipedia

Size: 3 inches (7.6 centimeters)

Ghost or burrowing shrimp are common inhabitants of the muddy bottom in the intertidal zone. They have elaborate tunnels that connect with other individuals in their colony.

They eat detritus, or non-living organic fragments of various critters.

Ghost shrimp are a favorite treat of gray whales. The earlier gray whale photo shows them scooping up bottom sediment in order to feed on these shrimp.

Spot Shrimp
Pandalus platyceros

Dan Clements

Size: 9.8 inches (25 centimeters)

This is the largest shrimp in Puget Sound, and its nocturnal behavior and preference for deep water make it difficult to find adults in the Park.

Juveniles frequent the Park, and change colors from green to brown to red to match the background colors of the algae, kelp, or seaweed where they are hiding.

Spot shrimp live for approximately four years and, like coonstripe, switch from male to female.

Chitons, Clams, Mussels, Scallops, & Snail Creatures

On-line:
  http://en.wikipedia.org/
  http://www.sealifebase.org/
  http://olympiccoast.noaa.gov/
  http://www.springerlink.com/

Print:
  Whales to Whelks by Rick Harbo
  Marine Life of the Pacific Northwest by Andy Lamb

Blue Line Chiton
Tonicella undocaerulea

Kirt L. Onthank, Wikipedia

Size: 2 inches (5 centimeters)

The psychedelic appearing blue lined chiton has a file like tongue (radula) which it uses to scrape food from the rocks and features where it attaches itself. While these species have been known to live up to 18 years, their average life span is five years.

Their diet consists of small diatoms, bryazoans and crustaceans that they remove from the coralline algae covering rocks. Predators include several species of sea star, harlequin ducks, and river otter.

Gumboot Chiton
Cryptochiton stelleri

Derek Holzapfel, Naturediver

Size: 9.8 inches (25 centimeters)

The largest chiton in the world, the gumboot chiton is named after its similar color and texture to the reddish brown sole of a rubber boot.

These chiton grow very slowly: those larger than six inches are at least 20 years old, and they may live 25 years or longer.

Major predators include river otter, and tidepool sculpin. Home ranges are very limited, as these chiton move less than 60 feet in a year.

Hairy Chiton
Mopalia ciliata

Tanya Dewey, Animal Diversity Web

Size: 3.9 inches (10 centimeters)

As their name implies, these chiton are covered in hair to make them more tolerant of sunlight. They feed at night, and firmly attach themselves to rocks at low tide.

In the process of scraping food off of rocks they pick-up magnetite, and as a result their mouths can become magnetic. They not only eat algae, they also dine on animals like sponges, bryozoans, and hydroids. Hairy chiton can live 20 years or longer.

Lined Chiton
Tonicella lineata

Dan Clements

Size: 2 inches (5 centimeters)

This chiton is distinguished by brown lines that squiggle over a colorful background of gold, pink, and green or blue.

The lined chiton is most commonly found on the jetty rocks where it feeds on pink-colored algae and tiny organisms who live in the algae.

This chiton has a twenty year life span, and is a favorite food of several sea star. Look for this chiton hidden among rocks on the jetty.

Mossy Chiton
Mopalia muscosa

Derek Holzapfel, Naturediver

Size: 3.9 inches (10 centimeters)

While most chitons are plant eaters, the mossy chiton eats animals including sponges, bryozoans, and hydroids. They are nocturnal feeders, and dine only when covered by water.

Mossy chiton have "home scars," or places on rocks where they return after feeding excursions. Their feeding area is usually within 20 inches of their "home scar."

Look for them on the rocks that form the jetty.

Butter or Long Neck Clam
Saxidomus giganteus

Oregon Department of Fish and Wildlife

Size: To 5.3 inches (13 centimeters)

Butter clams are common throughout the Park, but are most numerous in the lower intertidal area. They typically bury themselves 12" into sandy bottoms. These clams can live up to 20 years.

Predators include Dungeness crab, sunflower sea star, moon snail, various seabirds, and man. Butter clam's diet consists of plankton that is removed from the water by siphon tips on its feeding tube. Indigenous peoples of Puget Sound used butter neck clam shells as currency.

Geoduck Clam
Panopea generosa

Owen Caddy, City of Edmonds Discovery Program

Size: Shell to 11 inches (27.9 centimeters)

The world's largest intertidal clam, geoducks have lived in the Pacific Northwest for over 25 million years. They bury themselves three feet into the bottom, so their shells are rarely seen in the Park. Divers may see their siphons.

With a life span of up to 168 years, the geoduck is one of the longest lived creatures on the planet. It can weigh as much as 20 pounds.

It dines on plankton that drift by its feeding siphon.

Horse Clam
Tresus nuttalli

Dan Clements

Size: Shell to 9 inches (23 centimeters)

This smaller relative of the geoduck can weigh up to four pounds, and buries itself 12-16 inches into the bottom substrate, so it is much easier to harvest than the geoduck.

This is the only Washington clam whose siphon (see photo above) is tipped with leathery flaps, frequently with barnacles and algae attached. It is estimated that horse clams can live up to 20 years.

Like their cousins, horse clams are plankton feeders.

Pacific Little Neck Clam
Protothaca staminea

Dan Clements

Size: 2.4 inches (6 centimeters)

Pacific little neck clams can be found throughout the Park's intertidal sandy and muddy bottom areas. They are shallow burrowers, and are generally no more than four inches below the surface.

Little necks are slow growers, taking four to six years to reach the commercial harvest size of two inches. In Puget Sound these clams have an estimated life of ten years. Because of their shallow burrow depth they are a favorite food of moon snails, sea star, and crab.

Heart Cockle
Clinocardium nuttalli

Johanna Raupe

Size: 5.5 inches (14 centimeters)

Heart cockles are regularly seen in the eelgrass and sandy flats east of the eelgrass beds. While they burrow just below the surface, they also appear on the bottom.

When they are out in the open, divers often see them being pursued by birds, moon snail, sunflower star, and pink star. They have an amazing escape mechanism where they extend their "foot" out of their shells and literally leap away or turn over and escape. They can live up to 16 years.

California Mussel
Mytilus californianus

Dan Clements

Size: To 10 inches (25 centimeters)

California mussels attach themselves to rocks on the jetty and other solid features in the Park. Its blue/black shell has radial ridges.

California mussels compete for space on sites like the jetty with blue mussels. Their survival strategy is based upon more rapid growth and low level spawning throughout the year. They live to 10 years.

Predators include sea stars, predatory snails, crabs, gulls, and man.

Pacific Blue Mussel
Mytilus trossulus

Andreas Trepte, Wikipedia

Size: To 6 inches (15 centimeters)

Pacific blue mussels attach themselves to rocks on the jetty and other solid features in the Park. In spite of its name, its smooth shell is black, blue-black, or brown in color.

These mussels live for one to two years in this region, while in other parts of the world their life spans increase to 17 years. They compete for space with California mussels, and use a strategy of growing more quickly, and spawning once a year.

Rough Piddock
Zirfaea pilsbryi

Dan Clements

Size: Shell 6 inches, body 25 inches (15/60 cm)

These clam type creatures burrow into the hard clay, and the tip of their body protrudes into the water (photo). Their brightly colored siphons filter water for food.

The rough piddock can live up to eight years, and spends its entire life in its burrow. When it dies other marine life such as sea anemone and crabs may take over its den. Look for them off the west end of the jetty.

Rock Scallop
Crassadoma gigantea

Steve Lonhart, NOAA, Wikipedia

Size: 10 inches (25 centimeters)

As a juvenile, rock scallops swim freely about the Park. When they grow to about a one inch size they attach themselves to hard surfaces where they can live for up to 50 years. They are often covered with marine organisms.

Rock scallops are suspension feeders who typically dine on phytoplankton, detritus, and zooplankton. They are preyed upon by sea star and shell boring organisms. Look for them on more permanent man-made features throughout the Park.

Lewis' Moon Snail
Polynices lewisii

Dan Clements

Size: To 12 inches (30.5 centimeters)

Lewis' moon snails are aggressive carnivores and are most commonly found in the sandy areas east of the eelgrass beds, and in eelgrass.

Adults consume approximately one clam every four days by drilling what appears to be a countersunk hole in the clam's hinge. They have beautiful circular nests, called "sand collars," that look like pottery. It is preyed upon by sunflower star. Moon snail shells are in high demand by larger hermit crabs.

Octopi & Squid Critters

For Additional Information:

On-line:
   http://en.wikipedia.org/
   http://www.sealifebase.org/
   http://olympiccoast.noaa.gov/
   http://www.springerlink.com/
   www.thecephalopodpage.org/

Print:
   Whales to Whelks by Rick Harbo
   Marine Life of the Pacific Northwest
     by Andy Lamb

Giant Pacific Octopus
Enteroctopus dofleini

R. N. Lea, NOAA, Wikipedia

Size: 24 foot Tentacle Span (7.3 meters)

The Pacific octopus is the largest octopus in the world. Highly intelligent and fast growing, they can weigh over 160 pounds. They are rare Park visitors.

These cephalapods change color to camouflage themselves. Males live for abouty four years, females for three. Females die shortly after laying eggs.

This species commonly preys on shrimp, crabs, scallops, clams, and fish, including sharks. Harbor seals and man are principal predators in Puget Sound.

Red Octopus
Octopus rubescens

Kirt L. Onthank, Wikipedia

Size: 20 inch Tentacle Span (50 centimeters)

The red octopus is the most commonly occurring shallow-water octopus in Puget Sound. They can change color and texture, making its appearance highly variable. Color can vary from a deep brick red, to brown, to white, or mottled mixtures of the three.

Look for them in nooks and crannies in features throughout the Park. Shell litter is a sign they may be present. They have a two to three year life span, and dine on a wide variety of gastropods, bivalves, crabs and barnacles. Fish and seals prey on them.

Stubby Squid
Rossia pacifica

Veronica von Allwörden, Sky and Sea Photography

Size: 4.3 inches (11 centimeters)

This nocturnal squid typically likes deeper water outside the Park boundary, and is therefore rarely seen. At night they may move into shallower water in search of food.

These small squid have a short life span of approximately 18 months. Shrimps, crabs, small fishes, and cephalopods are the major elements of this critter's diet. Divers enjoy seeing the stubby squid rise from the sand and release ink blobs during night dives.

Opal Squid
Loligo opalescens

Toddography, Wikipedia

Size: To 7.5 inches (19 centimeters)

While these squid can live up to three years, their normal life span is approximately 12-18 months. They are able to change colors to match their surroundings. Opal squid are not commonly seen in the Park, but their nests are quite visible. They look like groups of slender white sausages attached to solid Park features. This squid is a predator that feeds on small fish, molluscs, crabs, shrimp, worms, plankton, mysids, ephausids, and smaller squid.

Salmon, seals, birds, and man prey on opal squid.

Sea Stars, Urchins, & Sea Cucumber Critters

For Additional Information:

On-line:
   http://en.wikipedia.org/
   http://www.sealifebase.org/
   http://olympiccoast.noaa.gov/
   http://www.springerlink.com/
   www.ndc.noaa.gov/newsltr/
   http://racerocks.com/
   http://busybee.mba.ac.uk/

Print:
   Whales to Whelks by Rick Harbo
   Marine Life of the Pacific Northwest
     by Andy Lamb

Sea Cucumber
Parastichopus californicus

Dan Clements

Size: 20 inches (50 centimeters)

Frequently seen in the Park, the sea cucumber is a solitary nocturnal animal. It has the ability to regenerate all parts of its body.

When threatened, it can expel all its internal organs through its anus and grow new ones. It can also expel sticky filaments to ensnare or confuse predators. It is a scavenger that feeds on plankton and other organic material.

Sea cucumbers can live up to ten years.

Leather Star
Dermasterias imbricate

Johanna Raupe

Size: 12 inches (30 centimeters)

Like all sea stars, the leather star can greatly extend its mouth. For larger prey, the stomach can move outside the mouth to digest prey.

Slimy to touch, these creatures feel like wet suede leather because they lack the short spines found on other sea star species. Their life span is a subject of debate: some references indicate 40 years, others three to five. Their diet primarily consists of barnacles, mussels, anemones, and sea pens. They are found on the jetty and Park features.

Pacific Blood Star
Henricia leviuscula

Dan Clements

Size: To 13 inches (32 centimeters)

Blood stars are scavengers who are fond of rocks and features. They are not particularly picky eaters, as their diet includes plankton, sponges, coral, algae, bivalve mollusks, shrimp, marine snails, fish, anemones, worms, and detritus. Sea stars like the blood star have a unique way of eating clams and mussels. They insert a portion of their stomach into the shell. Enzymes are released and digest the fleshy part of the mollusk inside its own shell. The digested contents are moved back into the sea star leaving an empty bivalve shell.

Purple or Ochre Star
Pisaster ochraceus

Dan Clements

Size: To 20 inches (50 centimeters)

Purple star are carnivores and considered to be the principle predator of the Pacific Coast intertidal zone. It wraps its arms around clams, mussels, and other prey, and pries open the shell. It then inserts its stomach and begins digesting the victim.

Since sea stars regenerate lost limbs and organs, their longevity is a matter of debate. Some sources indicate they can live to 40 years, others three to five years. They have few predators. Look for them throughout the Park on rocks and features.

Rose Star
Crossaster papposus

Veronica von Allwörden, Sky and Sea Photography

Size: To 14 inches (34 centimeters)

This is a beautiful sea star, frequently showing concentric rings of bright red, orange, white, and yellow.

The rose star was studied extensively over a 17 year period, and it is known that these sea stars have life spans exceeding 20 years.

These highly mobile sea star have a diet primarily consisting of anemones, sea pens, urchins, and smaller sea stars.

Spiny Red Star
Hippasteria spinosa

Olympic Coast Nat'l Marine Sanctuary, NOAA

Size: To 13.5 inches (34 centimeters)

This somewhat rare sea star is quite beautiful, with colors ranging from orange to vermilion, growing in intensity toward the tips of its stubby arms.

Unlike many of its relatives, the spiny red sea star has a single dietary preference: sea pens. It will also feed on plumose anemones, worms, and tunicates.

This star prefers the Park's muddy, shallow environments, but can also be found on rock and man-made features.

Striped Sun Star
Solaster stimpsoni

Veronica von Allwörden, Sky and Sea Photography

Size: To 10 inches (25 centimeters)

This is the most common species of the many armed sun star, and is sufficiently agile to form a ball by curling its arms over its body. It can use this form of locomotion to roll along the sea floor with currents.

The striped sun star is a carnivore, with sea cucumbers at the top of its menu list. These critters also include tunicates, sea pens, sea squirts and nudibranchs in their diet. Its primary predator is the sunflower sea star. Look for it on the jetty, rocky bottom areas, and other Park features.

Sunflower Star
Pycnopodia helianthoides

Dan Clements

Size: To 32 inches (81.3 centimeters)

These are reputedly the largest sea stars in the world, and are common throughout the area. They also move surprisingly fast over the bottom: over three feet in a minute.

These stars normally have 24 arms supporting over 15,000 tubes! They have large appetites, and can be seen eating snails, clams, cockles, urchins, and other sea stars. They are extremely colorful, ranging from purple to brown to orange to yellow.

Vermilion Star
Mediaster aequalis

Dan Clements

Size: To 4 inches (10 centimeters)

One of the Park's smaller sea stars, the vermilion star is common in shallow subtidal water. It can be found throughout the Park on rocks, pebbles, and sandy bottoms. They can travel up to fifteen inches in a minute.

The vermilion's diet varies with the season and bottom composition. They eat sponges, bryozoans, and sea pen. They breed from March to May, and females may lay 1,800 eggs in a year.

Green Sea Urchin
Strongylocentrotus droebachiensis

Dan Clements

Size: 3.5 inches (9 centimeters)

Green sea urchins are one of the most widely distributed Echinoderms: circumpolar into the Arctic regions of both the Atlantic and Pacific Oceans, and from tide pools to depths of 3,600 feet.

The green urchin's diet primarily consists of dining on seaweed and kelp, but will also eat a wide variety of organisms including mussels, sand dollars, barnacles, and other sea urchins. They are preyed upon by crabs, sea stars, wolf eels and humans who like "uni". It is thought these creatures live up to 8 years.

Anemones, Jellies, & Sea Pen Creatures

For Additional Information:

On-line:
   http://en.wikipedia.org/
   http://www.sealifebase.org/
   http://olympiccoast.noaa.gov/
   http://www.racerocks.com/
   http://www.nwmarinelife.com/

Print:
   Whales to Whelks by Rick Harbo
   Marine Life of the Pacific Northwest
      by Andy Lamb

Brooding Anemone
Epiactis prolifera

Dan Clements

Size: 2 inches (5.1 centimeters)

These fascinating little anemones are very common, and are most easily seen attached to blades of eelgrass. They appear as small flowers, but on closer inspection divers can see their feeding arms searching for food.

While their color varies, greens and browns are the most common when attached to eelgrass, and pink or red when attached to rocks. They eat small crustaceans, shrimp, and fish. They are prey of several species of nudibranchs, sea stars, and fish.

Giant Green or Green Surf Anemone
Anthopleura xanthogrammica

Dan Clements

Size: 10 inches (25 centimeters)

The giant green anemone lives throughout the Park. It is most commonly seen on and around the jetty, and attached to permanent features in the Park.

There are thousands of stinging nematocysts on this anemone's tentacles. It uses stings to paralyze prey: detached mussels, crabs, sea urchins and small fish. Its most common predators are snails.

When exposed to sunlight they turn darker green due to algae living in it growing in number.

Painted Anemone
Urticina crassicornis

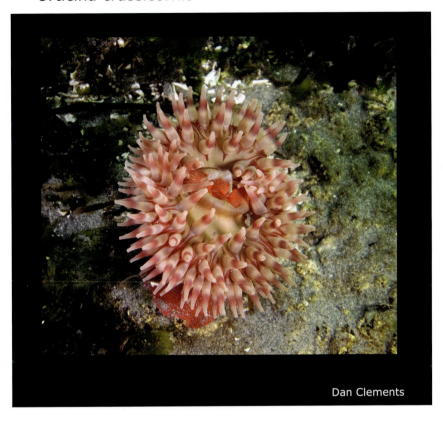

Dan Clements

Size: 3 inches (7.5 centimeters)

These beautiful anemone are extremely long lived. They have reported life spans of 60 to 80 years. They are most commonly seen attached to rock or man-made Park features.

A non-selective diner, painted anemone use their stinging abilities to paralyze small fish, crab, and molluscs, which they then consume. They are, in turn, menu items for sunflower and other stars, and marine gastropods. When attacked, they curl their tentacles inward and release stinging nematocysts.

Plumose Anemone
Metridium giganteum

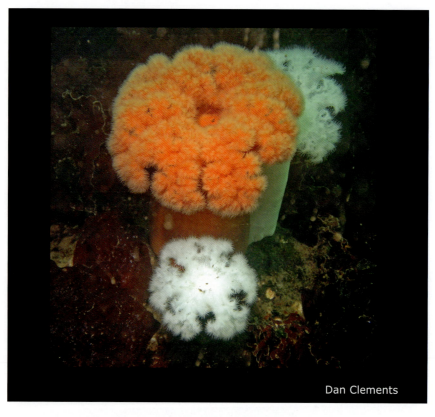
Dan Clements

Size: To 36 inches High (1 meter)

These large anemone attach themselves to rocks and man made features throughout the Park. They have extreme longevity, and reportedly can survive one to two hundred years.

Plumose anemone feed on plankton they capture with their stinging tentacles. Shaggy Nudibranchs and Leather Stars dine on these anemone.

Coloration in this critter varies from white to tan to brown to orange.

Short Plumose Anemone
Metridium senile

Veronica von Allwörden, Sky and Sea Photography

Size: To 4 inches High (10 centimeters)

These smaller versions of giant plumose anemone are commonly found in dense colonies where their color ranges from white, cream, brown, tan, and orange.

Reproduction is both sexual and asexual. In asexual development, when this anemone moves, small portions of the base are left, and these develop into another short plumose. Shaggy mouse nudibranchs and leather stars prey on these anemone. They feed on zooplankton, and pieces of fish and squid.

Tube Anemone
Pachycerianthus fimbriatus

Dan Clements

Size: To 12 inches (30 centimeters)

This unusual anemone burrows its semi-rigid secreted "mucous" base tube up to three feet into the Park's soft bottom areas. Look for tube anemone in the Park's sandy and muddy bottom areas. Coloration ranges from bright orange to red.

Like its relatives, tube anemone feed on plankton and small crustaceans. They are reported to be a favorite food of giant nudibranch. These nudibranch are known to lay egg masses on the hard tube that protects these anemone (photo above).

Fried Egg or Egg Yolk Jelly
Phacellophora camtschatica

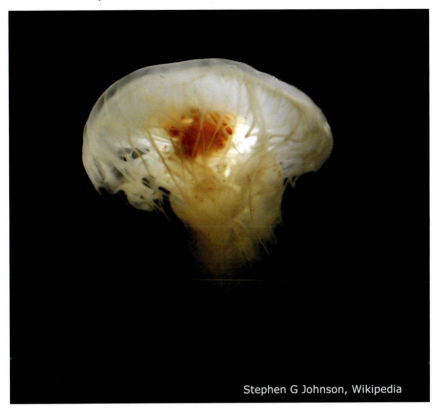

Stephen G Johnson, Wikipedia

Size: To 19.7 feet (6 meters)

This large jelly, with a two foot bell, is both a hunter and "public transportation" provider.

It feeds on smaller jellyfish and other gelatinous zooplankton, which become trapped in its tentacles. The sting of this jelly is weak, so small crustaceans regularly ride on its bell and even steal food from its tentacles.

Fried egg jellies grow quickly, and have a life span under one year.

Lion's Mane Jelly
Cyanea capillata

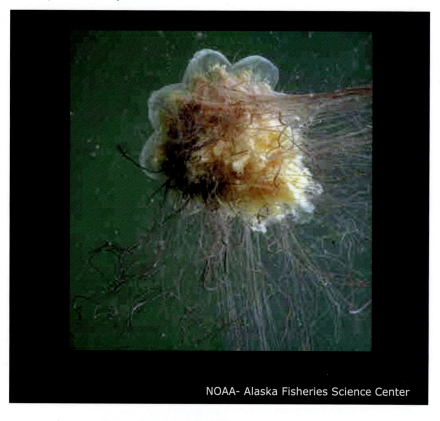

NOAA- Alaska Fisheries Science Center

Size: To 98 feet (30 meters)

The lion's mane jelly is the largest known specie of jelly. The largest recorded specimen had a seven foot, six inch bell, and was 120 feet long! Their sting is quite strong, and humans should avoid contact with this critter.

These jellies feed on zooplankton, small fish, and other jellies. In turn, lion's mane are preyed upon by seabirds, larger fish, other jellyfish species and sea turtles. They grow rapidly, and their longevity is less than one year.

Sarsia Jelly
Sarsia sp

Dan Clements

Size: 0.5 inches (12.5 millimeters)

On dives it is sometimes fun to stop and examine small objects floating in front of you. These small jellies hang motionless in the water and look like creatures from another world.

With their four tentacles hanging in the water below their bell, they feed on small planktonic crustaceans drifting by them.

They have a short life span of a few months, and are most commonly seen in the Park from spring to fall.

Water Jelly
Aequorea victoria

Dan Clements

Size: 5 inches (12.5 centimeters)

This common jelly gently undulates through the water. In the dark, they are luminescent. The 2008 Nobel prize in chemistry was awarded for bioluminescence research conducted on these creatures.

Water jellies typically feed on soft-bodied organisms, but their diet may include some crustacean zooplankton. They are on the dinner menu for lion's mane and other jellies.

They live about six months: from late spring to fall.

Sea Pen
Ptilosarcus gurneyi

BackpackPhotography, Wikipedia

Size: To 18 inches (46 centimeters)

Sea pen are related to coral, and feed off of plankton drifting in the water. Once common throughout Puget Sound, their numbers have declined in recent years. They are especially susceptible to environmental degradation.

If you look closely at an individual polyp on a sea pen, you will see it is comprised of eight small tentacles. They are called sea pens because of their resemblance to old style quill pens. They have a life span of 15 plus years.

Sea Slug & Worm Creatures

For Additional Information:

On-line:
   http://en.wikipedia.org/
   http://www.seaslugforum.net/
   http://academic.evergreen.edu/

Print:
   Whales to Whelks by Rick Harbo
   Marine Life of the Pacific Northwest
     by Andy Lamb
   Eastern Pacific Nudibranchs
     by David Behrens & Alicia Hermosillo

Red Dendronotid
Dendronotus rufus

Dan Clements

Size: 11 inches (28 centimeters)

This beautiful creature has a white, translucent body, with the tips of the cerata (growths from the body) colored magenta. There are six to nine pair of cerata, which is from the Greek word for horn (keratos).

This species was studied extensively in the 1970's, and little is known about its diet. It is believed they eat water jellies and hydroids. Jan Kocian on Whidbey Island has observed what is believed to be a red dendronotid defending its egg mass from star fish using chemical scent. They live about a year.

Gold Dirona
Dirona pellucida

Dan Clements

Size: 4.7 inches (12 centimeters)

This striking nudibranch ranges in color from red to golden orange with frosted cerata tips.

It is a fairly common sight throughout the Park. Look for it in the eelgrass beds, in plant growth along the rope trails, and on sandy bottom areas.

Surviving a year, these nudibranchs dine on bryozoans, or small animals that build calcium carbonate skeletons, and hydroids. Until 1997 this species was known as Dirona aurantia in North America.

Alabaster or White Line Nudibranch
Dirona albolineata

Dan Clements

Size: To 7 inches (17.5 centimeters)

If you take your camera into the Park, alabaster nudibranchs are an irresistible photo subject. These beautiful translucent animals are extremely common, and may be seen clinging to plant growth or on the sandy bottom. They have a life span of approximately twelve months.

They tend to favor bryozoans (small calcium carbonate building creatures), and small snails for their dining pleasure. They have strong jaws for crushing and consuming their prey.

Brown Striped Nudibranch
Armina californica

Minette Layne, Wikipedia

Size: To 3 inches (7.5 centimeters)

This small critter likes the Park's sandy and muddy bottom areas where it searches out its favorite meal of orange sea pens. They have few predators.

Brown striped nudibranchs are nighttime hunters, and are rarely seen during daylight hours. While the sun is up they bury themselves in the sand or mud.

Like all nudibranchs, they are hermaphroditic, having both male and female sex organs. When mating they can be seen side by side. They live a year.

Hooded or Lion's Mane Nudibranch
Melibe leonina

Johanna Raupe

Size: To 4 inches (10 centimeters)

The strange hooded nudibranch is almost transparent, and has a slight yellowish-green cast. Unlike other nudibranchs, they have no radula ("teeth") or jaws. It uses its oral hood, lined with 2 rows of tentacles to capture prey.

Look for these nudibranchs in the Park's eelgrass beds. It is a hunter whose diet includes small crustaceans and post-larval mollusks. They are a favorite meal of kelp crabs. They live for approximately one year.

Opalescent or Horned Nudibranch
Hermissenda crassicornis

Dan Clements

Size: To 3.2 inches (8 centimeters)

These small, delicate, beautiful nudibranchs are a favorite of Park photographers. This common resident is most frequently encountered in the Park's eelgrass beds (above on an eelgrass blade) and in the plants near the rope trail system.

Like other nudibranchs, this species is hermaphroditic, and lives for about a year. They feed on marine invertebrate hydroids and other nudibranchs. The orange color highlights and stinging cerata act as this creature's main defense mechanisms.

Shaggy or Mouse Nudibranch
Aeolidia papillosa

Minette Layne, Wikipedia

Size: To 4 inches (10 centimeters)

The shaggy nudibranch is the Park's equivalent of MacGyver. Not only does it feed on various types of sea anemone, it places the anemone's undischarged stinging nematocyst cells in its cerata to protect it from predation by other creatures.

And how do they avoid the anemone's stings? They secrete a compound that discharges the anemone's nematocysts before they affect the shaggy nudibranch. These critters live for about twelve months, and are hermaphroditic.

Monterey Sea Lemon Nudibranch
Doris montereyensis

Dan Clements

Size: To 6 inches (15 centimeters)

This nudibranch and its egg masses get their yellow coloration from the sponges that it preys upon. It is common throughout the Park, and may be seen on the bottom, on kelp, or on features.

Like other nudibranchs, Monterey sea lemon are hermaphroditic and carry both male and female reproductive organs. They can be observed mating when they are parallel next to each other.

They have a life span of approximately one year.

Nanaimo Nudibranch
Acanthodoris nanaimoensis

Veronica von Allwörden, Sky and Sea Photography

Size: 1.5 inches (4 centimeters)

Nanaimo nudibranchs range in color from a beautiful translucent white pictured above to grey. They are not commonly seen in the Park, but prefer rocky areas and hard man-made features.

These critters have a short life span of approximately one year. This nudibranch species dines on compound tunicates like sea squirts, and bryozoans, or creatures who construct calcium carbonate colonies. They are hermaphroditic, possessing both male and female reproductive organs.

Ring Spotted Nudibranch
Diaulula sandiegensis

Dan Clements

Size: To 5 inches (12.5 centimeters)

Also known as Leopard Dorids, these nudibranchs vary in color from white to orange. Their contrasting "rings" are a beautiful light brown.

These common Park residents most frequently dine on sponges. They can be found on kelp growth that parallels rope marked trails, on rocky bottom, and hard surfaced man-made features and structures.

Ring spotted dorids' longevity is about twelve months.

Diamond Back Tritonia
Tritonia festiva

Veronica von Allwörden, Sky and Sea Photography

Size: To 4 inches (10 centimeters)

Diamond back tritonia are opportunistic predators who feed on the Park's soft coral and Sea Pen. They can be found on rocks, and sandy/muddy bottom areas.

This nudibranch has the ability of escaping predators like predatory sunflower stars by swimming off the bottom and away to safety. They live approximately one year, and like other nudibranchs have male and female reproductive organs.

Spotted Aglajid
Aglaja ocelligera

Johanna Raupe

Size: 1 inch (2.5 centimeters)

The spotted aglajid can be found in the Park during summer and fall months. Look for it on shallow, soft bottom areas where sea lettuce is found. During spring months these critters can sometimes be seen out of the water on sand during low tides.

Underwater these nudibranchs appear brown with little color. When they are lit up with lights or strobes their beautiful blue highlights appear. Like most nudibranchs, their life span is less than one year.

Breadcrumb Sponge
Halichondria bowerbanki

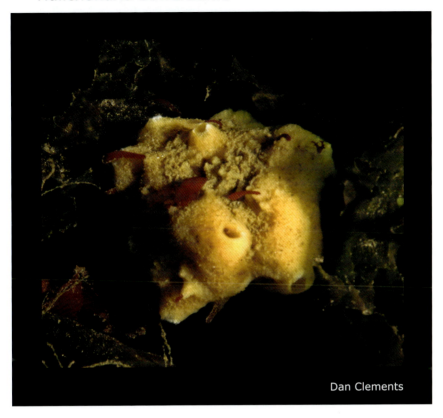

Size: To 12 inches (30.5 centimeters) in Park

Bread crumb sponges' coloration varies from beige to dull brown during summer months, to light grey/yellow during winter. They turn yellow to orange when spawning.

This sponge is a common menu item for several types of nudibranchs and fish. They feed on organic material suspended in the water.

The estimated life span for a bread crumb sponge is three years, which it spends in a single location.

Phyllodoce Worm
Phyllodoce spp

Johanna Raupe

Size: This individual 12 inches (30 centimeters)

This unidentified worm appears to be a type of phyllodoce. Attempts to identify this critter with staff of the Seattle and Monterey Aquariums were unsuccessful.

This subject was photographed in the Park's relatively shallow sandy bottom area. .

Because of the lack of positive identification, no information regarding life span, diet, or predators is available.

Calcareous Tube Worm
Serpula vermicularis

Dan Clements

Size: 2.5 inches (6.5 centimeters)

Coloration in the calcereous tube worm can vary from a brilliant red to orange to pink to white, and is always spectacular. The worm attaches its hard tube home to solid surfaces like rocks, sunken boats, and other features throughout the Park.

This critter enjoys playing hide and seek with underwater photographers: a diver's movement causes them to retract into their tubes. Large nerve fibers running through their bodies give them rapid retraction speed. They have a two to five year life span.

Feather Duster Worm
Eudistylia vancouveri

Owen Caddy, City of Edmonds Discovery Program

Size: To 24 inches (60 centimeters)

These shy creatures are difficult to photograph. When they sense the slightest movement or shadow they retreat into parchment tubes formed by their secretions.

They are a common sight in the Park and tend to form large colonies on rocks and man-made features. They feed by collecting food from the water with their "feather duster" cirri. They are able to retract so quickly into their tubes because they have a long nerve that runs the length of their body.

Orange Ribbon Worm
Carinella speciosa

Johanna Raupe

Size: To 39 inches (1 meter)

This spectacular orange worm is a solid color without bands or stripes. It is most commonly spotted in the Park's shallow, subtidal areas.

This species may eat small crustaceans as well as annelid worms and may be found searching for food at low tide. When this worm is contracted, it may be as thick around as a pencil. It is commonly found stretched out.

Females lay eggs in summer.

Six Lined Ribbon Worm
Carinella sexlineatus

Johanna Raupe

Size: To 39 inches (1 meter)

This worm likes the Park's shallow intertidal and subtidal areas east of the eelgrass. Look for it on the jetty and solid man-made features among mussels and algae.

This striking worm is easy to identify because of its dark brown coloration, six lines that run the length of its body, and white bands that ring it. Since the six lined ribbon worm moves about in the open, it is a common sight for divers. Its diet includes polychaetes and other marine invertebrates.

Eelgrass, Seaweed, and Kelp

For Additional Information:

On-line:
  http://en.wikipedia.org/
  http://www.ecy.wa.gov/
  http://www.freepatentsonline.com
  http://www.beachwatchers.wsu.edu
  http://www.mbari.org/
  http://dnr.metrokc.gov/wlr/

Print:
  Marine Life of the Pacific Northwest
    by Andy Lamb

Eelgrass
Zostera marina

Dan Clements

Size: 6.6 feet (2 meters) long, 0.5 inch wide.

Eelgrass beds are some of the most important areas in the Park. This plant grows in relatively shallow areas and attaches itself to the bottom in sandy or muddy areas. Eelgrass "meadows" grow in the sunlight of spring and summer, then decay in the fall and winter months.

Eelgrass helps prevent erosion, and provides food and shelter for a wide variety of fish, marine invertebrates, and birds.

Bull Kelp
Nereocystis luetkeana

Dan Clements

Size: To 118 feet (36 meters)

This annual seaweed grows quite rapidly, and reaches its full height by June. They are attached to deeper bottom areas in the Park by numerous haptera, or finger-like projections. While some Bull Kelp may survive into a second season, winter storms dislodge them from the bottom.

This kelp provides an important environment for other plants and animals. Indigenous peoples of the Pacific Northwest used the bulbs as containers for water and fish oil.

Seersucker Kelp
Costaria costata

Rhoda H Green

Size: To 10 feet (3 meters)

This kelp is distinguished by the five distinct ribs running the length of the blade. It also has a very blistered appearance.

This species has two different forms: plants growing in exposed areas grow long and thin, while plants in more sheltered waters grow broad and short.

Seersucker kelp is common throughout the Park from spring through fall. Look for specimens along the trail rope lines beyond the eelgrass beds.

Sugar Kelp or Sugar Wrack
Laminaria saccharina

Rhoda H Green

Size: To 10 feet (3 meters)

Sugar kelp is identified by the blister like ripples running down each side of the blade. Very young and older specimens may lack these blisters, or "bullations." It is common along the rope marked trails.

Sugar kelp attaches itself to the bottom by use of a holdfast: a root like structure that connects it to rocks, shells, and other debris. Unlike many plants, holdfasts do not help provide food for the kelp, and are not true roots. Their role is simply to hold the plant in place.

Delicate Sea Lace
Microcladia coulteri

Dan Clements

Size: To 16 inches (40 centimeters)

Sea lace is a delicate red algae that grows both on the bottom and on various types of kelp: predominantly on large red algae, and occasionally on large brown algae. It is commonly seen in shallow areas of the Park west of the eelgrass beds.

Interestingly, the delicate sea lace is being used as a nutritional supplement by aquaculturists to increase growth rates in shellfish like abalone and oysters.

Sea Lettuce
Ulva lactuca

Rhoda H Green

Size: To 39 inches (1 meter)

Sea lettuce is one of the most common plants in the Park, and it is almost impossible to exit the water after a dive in the summer months without copious amounts hanging from equipment. It both attaches itself to the bottom, and also floats freely about.

This green algae is a member of the family that makes up an estimated 50% of all living matter on the planet. As such, it is a key provider of food source and habitat for much marine life. It is also edible, and an excellent protein and vitamin C source.

Blue Branching Seaweed
Fauchea laciniata

Veronica von Allwörden, Sky and Sea Photography

Size: 6.2 inches (15.5 centimeters)

Blue branching seaweed is a red algae whose leaves appear a beautiful greenish yellow or violet blue. This is caused by light reflecting off of gland cells on the surface of the plant.

It is common throughout the Park, especially along or on rope trail guides.

As is the case with other plants in the Park, blue branching seaweed provides both food and shelter for many fish and marine invertebrates.

Succulent Seaweed
Sarcodiotheca gaudichaudii

Rhoda H Green

Size: To 18 inches (45 centimeters)

Succulent seaweed look like a package of translucent noodles. This red algae is common throughout the Park. Look for it along the eastern end of Jetty Way trail. It is also known as red string seaweed.

Its color varies from deep red to straw yellow in summer when bleached by sunlight. It attaches itself to the bottom or Park feature by use of a tissue pad called a "holdfast."

This is another nutritious, edible plant.

Hairy Pottery Seaweed
Ceramium pacificum

Mandy Lindeberg, Seaweeds of Alaska

Size: To 7 inches (18 centimeters)

Hairy pottery seaweed is a red algae that is pinkish/purple in color. It grows in lacy strings that form what appear to be small bushes. They are found in shallow areas east of the eelgrass beds.

This seaweed appears to have a life span of approximately one year. It is also interesting to note it has some defense against plant eaters by virtue of having sulfur in its cells. This plant is quite tolerant of changes in salinity and water temperature.

Wireweed
Sargassum muticum

Dan Clements

Size: To 6.6 feet (2 meters)

Wireweed is a brown algae. The spherical floats are the reproductive structures. It is a non-native species originating in Japan. It appeared in the 1930's.

There is debate on whether to consider it an invasive or not, as it provides good habitat for juvenile fish. Many adult fish choose it over other seaweeds to lay there eggs on. It is common throughout the Park.

With a life span of three to four years, Wireweed is one of the longer lived plants in the Park.

Bibliography

On Line:

Beneath a Tranquil Seas: http://www.chateaugris.com/BATS/
Birds on the Bay: http://www.birdsonthebay.ca/pdf_files/eelgrass_brochure_may06.pdf
ElasmoDiver.com: http://www.elasmodiver.com/BCMarinelife/BCML%20cnidaria.htm
e-Nature.com: http://www.enature.com/fieldguides/
FishBase: http://fishbase.org/search.php
Fishes of Puget Sound: http://www.uwfishcollection.org/FishKey/
JelliesZone: http://jellieszone.com/
Marine Life at the Cove: http://marinespeciespugetsound.com/Home.htm
Monterey Bay Aquarium Online Field Guide: http://www.mbayaq.org/efc/living_species/default.asp?hOri=1
NOAA Olympic Coast Marine Sanctuary: http://olympiccoast.noaa.gov/living/marine_wildlife/
Sea and Sky Sealinks: http://www.seasky.org/links/sealink02.html
Sea Slug Forum: http://www.seaslugforum.net/
SeaOtter Marine Life Index: http://www.seaotter.com/
Wikipedia: http://en.wikipedia.org/wiki/Main_Page

Print:

Coast Fish Identification: California to Alaska, Paul Humann, 1996
Eastern Pacific Nudibranchs, David W Behrens and Alicia Hermosillo, 2005
Edmonds Underwater Park Vegetation Survey, Pentec Environmental, December 5, 2005
Exploring the Seashore, Gloria Snively, 1989.
Marine Life of the Pacific Northwest, Andy Lamb and Bernard Hanby, 2005.

Index

Acanthodoris nanaimoensis 111
Acorn, or Giant Acorn, Barnacle 48
Aeolidia papillosa 109
Aequorea victoria 100
Aglaja ocelligera 114
Alabaster/White Line Nudibranch 105
Ammodytes hexapterus 36
Anthopleura xanthogrammica 92
Armina californica 106
Artedius harringtoni 41
Aulorhynchus flavidus 45

Balanus nubilis 48
Bay Goby 18
Blackeye Goby 19
Black Rockfish 30
Blue Branching Seaweed 128
Blue Line Chiton 59
Breadcrumb Sponge 115
Brooding Anemone 91
Brown Striped Nudibranch 106
Buffalo Sculpin 38
Bull Kelp 123
Butter or Long Neck Clam 64

Cabezon 16
Calcareous Tube Worm 117
California Mussel 69
California Sea Lion 12
Callianassa californiensis 56
Canary Rockfish 31
Cancer magister 50
Cancer productus 53
Carinella sexlineatus 120
Carinella speciosa 119
Ceramium pacificum 130
China Rockfish 32
Chirolophis decoratus 46
Citharichthys stigmaeus 37
Clinocardium nuttalli 68
Clupea pallasii 23
Coho or Silver Salmon 35
Coonstripe or Dock Shrimp 55
Copper Rockfish 33
Coryphopterus nicholsii 19
Costaria costata 124
Crassadoma gigantea 72
Crossaster papposus 84
Cryptochiton stelleri 60
Cyanea capillata 98
Cymatogaster aggregata 26

Decorated Warbonnet 46
Decorator Crab 49
Delicate Sea Lace 126
Dendronotus rufus 103
Dermasterias imbricate 81
Diamond Back Tritonia 113
Diaulula sandiegensis 112
Dirona albolineata 105
Dirona pellucida 104
Doris montereyensis 110
Dungeness Crab 50

Eelgrass 122
Embiotoca lateralis 42
Enophrys bison 38
Enteroctopus dofleini 75
Epiactis prolifera 91
Eschrichtius robustus 14
Eudistylia vancouveri 118

Fauchea laciniata 128
Feather Duster Worm 118
Fried Egg or Egg Yolk Jelly 97

Ghost Shrimp 56
Giant Green/Green Surf Anemone 92
Giant Pacific Octopus 75
Geoduck Clam 65
Gold Dirona 104
Green Sea Urchin 89
Gray Whale 14
Grunt Sculpin 39
Gumboot Chiton 60

Hairy Chiton 61
Hairy Pottery Seaweed 130
Halichondria bowerbanki 115
Harbor Seal 13
Heart Cockle 68
Hemilepidotus hemilepidotus 29
Henricia leviuscula 82
Hermissenda crassicornis 108
Hermit Crab 51
Hippasteria spinosa 85
Homo sapien scubenses 10
Hooded/ Lion's Mane Nudibranch 107
Horse Clam 66
Human Beings 10
Humpy or Pink Salmon 34
Hydrolagus colliei 28

Index, Continued

Kelp Crab 52

Laminaria saccharina 125
Leather Star 81
Lepidasthenia longicirrata 116
Lepidogobius lepidus 18
Lepidopsetta bilineata 44
Lewis' Moon Snail 73
Lined Chiton 62
Lingcod 24
Lion's Mane Jelly 98
Loligo opalescens 78
Long Fin Gunnel 21
Longnose Skate 43
Lontra canadensis 11
Lycodes palearis 17

Mediaster aequalis 88
Melibe leonina 107
Metridium giganteum 94
Metridium senile 95
Microcladia coulteri 126
Monterey Sea Lemon Nudibranch 110
Mopalia ciliata 61
Mopalia muscosa 63
Mossy Chiton 63
Munida quadrispina 54
Mytilus californianus 69
Mytilus trossulus 70

Nanaimo Nudibranch 111
Nautichthys oculofasciatus 40
Nereocystis luetkeana 123

Octopus rubescens 76
Oncorhynchus gorbuscha 34
Oncorhynchus kisutch 35
Opalescent or Horned Nudibranch 108
Opal Squid 78
Ophiodon elongates 24
Orange Ribbon Worm 119
Oregonia gracilis 49
Oxylebius pictus 20

Pachycerianthus fimbriatus 96
Pacific Blood Star 82
Pacific Blue Mussel 70
Pacific Herring 23
Pacific Little Neck Clam 67
Pacific Sand Lance 36
Pagurus beringanus 51

Painted Anemone 93
Painted Greenling 20
Pandalus danae 55
Pandalus platyceros 57
Panopea generosa 65
Parastichopus californicus 80
Phacellophora camtschatica 97
Phoca vitulina 13
Pholis clemensi 21
Pholis ornate 22
Phyllodoce Scaleworm 116

Pile Perch 25
Pisaster ochraceus 83
Plumose Anemone 94
Polynices lewisii 73
Protothaca staminea 67
Ptilichthys goodei 27
Ptilosarcus gurneyi 101
Pugettia gracilis 52
Purple or Ochre Star 83
Pycnopodia helianthoides 87

Quillfish 27

Raja rhina 43
Red Dendronotid 103
Red Irish Lord 29
Red Octopus 76
Red Rock Crab 53
Rhacochilus vacca 25
Rhamphocottus richardsonii 39
Ring Spotted Nudibranch 112
River Otter 11
Rock Scallop 72
Rock Sole 44
Rose Star 84
Rossia pacifica 77
Rough Piddock 71

Saddleback Gunnel 22
Sailfin Sculpin 40
Sarcodiotheca gaudichaudii 129
Sargassum muticum 131
Sarsia Jelly 99
Sarsia sp 99
Saxidomus giganteus 64
Scalyhead Sculpin 41
Scorpaenichthys marmoratus 16
Sea Cucumber 80
Sea Lettuce 127

Index, Continued

Sea Pen 101
Sebastes caurinus 33
Sebastes melanops 30
Sebastes nebulosus 32
Sebastes pinniger 31
Seersucker Kelp 124
Serpula vermicularis 117
Shaggy or Mouse Nudibranch 109
Shiner Perch 26
Short Plumose Anemone 95
Six Lined Ribbon Worm 120
Solaster stimpsoni 86
Speckled Sanddab 37
Spiney Red Star 85
Spot Shrimp 57
Spotted Aglajid 114
Spotted Ratfish 28
Squat Lobster 54
Striped Seaperch 42
Striped Sun Star 86
Strongylocentrotus droebachiensis 89
Stubby Squid 77

Succulent Seaweed 129
Sugar Kelp or Sugar Wrack 125
Sunflower Star 87

Tonicella lineata 62
Tonicella undocaerulea 59
Tresus nuttalli 66
Tritonia festiva 113
Tube Anemone 96
Tube-snout 45

Ulva lactuca 127
Urticina crassicornis 93

Vermilion Star 88

Water Jelly 100
Wattled Eelpouts 17
Wireweed 131

Zalophus californianus 12
Zirfaea pilsbryi 71
Zostera marina 122

Dan Clements

Dan is an adventurer who has a deep appreciation and respect for the world's natural wonders, and life in its many varied forms. He has climbed, skied, sailed, SCUBA dived, and traveled throughout the world.

When he is not underwater photographing he enjoys back country skiing, distance running, mountain biking, and opera. Everett, Washington is home base.